YOUR KNOWLEDGE HAS VALUE

- We will publish your bachelor's and master's thesis, essays and papers

- Your own eBook and book - sold worldwide in all relevant shops

- Earn money with each sale

Upload your text at www.GRIN.com
and publish for free

Clare Stalder

"It's getting dark on old Broadway". African American theatre of the Harlem Renaissance in search of the right direction

GRIN Verlag

Bibliografische Information der Deutschen Nationalbibliothek:

Die Deutsche Bibliothek verzeichnet diese Publikation in der Deutschen Nationalbibliografie; detaillierte bibliografische Daten sind im Internet über http://dnb.d-nb.de/ abrufbar.

Dieses Werk sowie alle darin enthaltenen einzelnen Beiträge und Abbildungen sind urheberrechtlich geschützt. Jede Verwertung, die nicht ausdrücklich vom Urheberrechtsschutz zugelassen ist, bedarf der vorherigen Zustimmung des Verlages. Das gilt insbesondere für Vervielfältigungen, Bearbeitungen, Übersetzungen, Mikroverfilmungen, Auswertungen durch Datenbanken und für die Einspeicherung und Verarbeitung in elektronische Systeme. Alle Rechte, auch die des auszugsweisen Nachdrucks, der fotomechanischen Wiedergabe (einschließlich Mikrokopie) sowie der Auswertung durch Datenbanken oder ähnliche Einrichtungen, vorbehalten.

Imprint:

Copyright © 2011 GRIN Verlag GmbH
Druck und Bindung: Books on Demand GmbH, Norderstedt Germany
ISBN: 978-3-656-41548-0

This book at GRIN:

http://www.grin.com/en/e-book/212985/it-s-getting-dark-on-old-broadway-african-american-theatre-of-the-harlem

GRIN - Your knowledge has value

Der GRIN Verlag publiziert seit 1998 wissenschaftliche Arbeiten von Studenten, Hochschullehrern und anderen Akademikern als eBook und gedrucktes Buch. Die Verlagswebsite www.grin.com ist die ideale Plattform zur Veröffentlichung von Hausarbeiten, Abschlussarbeiten, wissenschaftlichen Aufsätzen, Dissertationen und Fachbüchern.

Visit us on the internet:

http://www.grin.com/

http://www.facebook.com/grincom

http://www.twitter.com/grin_com

"It's getting dark on old Broadway"

African American theatre of the Harlem Renaissance in search of the right direction

Contents

Introduction 2

1 Blackface minstrelsy: the ancestors of Black theatre 3

2 Black musical theatre: From Broadway to Harlem nightclubs and back 4

    2.1 The special role of musical theatre 4

    2.2 Vaudeville and the first black musical comedies (1880-1910) 5

    2.3 The Term of Exile (1910-1920) 7

    2.4 Shuffle Along - Back to Broadway (1921-1929) 7

3 Black Drama: In search of the right direction 8

    3.1 Protest drama or folk theatre? 8

    3.2 Folk drama and the Little Theatre movement 10

    3.3 Black drama on Broadway 11

4 Dilemmas of the Black performer: dangers and chances of going mainstream 12

    4.1 The double audience 12

    4.2 Imitating white material or creating new black material 13

    4.3 White writers and producers staging "black" drama 14

    4.4 Segregation and discrimination 15

Conclusion 15

Introduction

> It's getting very dark on Old Broadway
> You see the change in ev'ry cabaret
> Just like an eclipse of the moon,
> Ev'ry café now has the dancing coon.
> Pretty choc'late ladies
> Shake and shimmie ev'rywhere
> Real dark-town entertainers hold the stage,
> You must black up to be the latest rage
> ("It's getting dark on old Broadway" from
> the *Ziegfeld Follies of 1922*, qtd. in Woll 76)

When Gilda Gray performed "It's Getting Dark on Old Broadway" in the opening show of the song-and-dance revue *Ziegfeld Follies* on 5 June 1922 she eternalized Broadway's latest trend (Woll 76). Black entertainment proliferated in the Theatre District along Broadway in the 1920s and it seemed that black shows had made it into the limelight of success. There was, however, a different 'dark' side to the developments of the black performance scene.

To many leading intellectuals of the Harlem Renaissance, the new darkness on Broadway looked rather bleak. Important figures like W. E. B. Du Bois who campaigned for a new racial identity through cultural creation (cf. Du Bois "Criteria of Negro Art") feared that the new phenomenon of black productions reaching out for mainstream success would betray their cause. In his speech at the NAACP's annual conference, he famously claimed that "all Art is propaganda and ever must be" (Du Bois par. 29). Catering to the white public's demands (pars. 33, 35), as the successful Black Broadway musicals did, would mean failing the cause, according to Du Bois. While some scholars argue that theatre and performance in the New Negro era played "a pivotal role in the evolution of Black Nationalism" (Krasner 1), those are opposed by a number of authors who look upon the Harlem Renaissance as a failure (cf. Baker xiii, Neal 39, Krasner 95f.).

In the following paper, I will look into the question of whether the performers and artists of the Harlem Renaissance really failed to contribute to a change of white America's attitude toward the African American race (Krasner 14). One point at issue will be whether the increasing success and commercialisation of Black theatre counteracted the objectives of racial renewal or if on the contrary, they were a means to an end.

In order to analyse what circumstances playwrights and performers had to overcome, I will outline the development of Black theatre since the 19th century. As Harlem Renaissance intellectuals aimed to put the biased images behind them, it is necessary to investigate thoroughly what these images were and where they came from. Hence, I will start my analysis by looking at minstrelsy and its influences on early Black musical theatre. Black dramatists and drama theorists were still struggling to reach a consensus on the issue of mainstream whereas musical theatre eventually cut its own path to commercial success on Broadway. This controversy will be summarised in chapter 3. Subsequently, I will research the seemingly unresolvable dilemmas Black artists had to deal with in order to eventually be able to evaluate the achievements and failures of the Harlem Renaissance theatre.

Theatre and performance were not chosen as the subject of discussion at random. In fact, oral and musical expression have always been at the centre of African American culture (Scott 427). Performance was the primary mode of communication when literature and written language in general were not available to the oppressed African Americans during times of slavery (Krasner 11). When Du Bois produced his pageant *Star of Ethiopia* in 1911, he was convinced that theatre was "the most accessible medium" for the purpose of changing the standing of the African American race (Hay 2).

Although musical theatre and drama had to deal with some genre-specific problems both genres need to be taken into account when assessing the impact of the performing arts. I will not include the role of dance in this study as this would mean to extend the topic to questions of gender roles and gender stereotypes.

1 Blackface minstrelsy: the ancestors of Black theatre

The Black artists of the Harlem Renaissance suffered from a heavy legacy. Not only did they have to "remove the mask of racial stereotypes" (Buck 795) in the figurative sense. At the beginning of the 20th century, white audiences had become accustomed to and appreciative of minstrel shows, in which blacks and whites performed songs and dances in burnt cork blackface. Minstrelsy and the blackface 'mask' became a byword for racial stereotypes and discrimination (cf. Mahar 5-6; Kenrick). Houston A. Baker Jr. describes the minstrel mask as a "space of habitation ... for that deep-seated denial of the indisputable humanity of ... descendants from the continent of Africa" (17). Baker goes so far as to refer to the minstrel mask as a symbol which was designed to remind whites of the inferiority of African Americans, an inferiority which makes them "fit for lynching" (21). The only theme of minstrel shows was in fact the ridicule and thus humiliation of Blacks. Black people were shown as dim-witted buffoons who spent their days doing nothing but singing and dancing (cf. Kenrick).

In the 1830s, white minstrel performer Thomas Darthmouth Rice became famous for his representation of Jim Crow. The number was a typical minstrel act: In blackface, Rice acted the role of a black slave. He performed a song and dance, the "Jumpin' Jim Crow", the steps of which he had supposedly learnt from a slave (Baker 19). The representation of Jim Crow became famous. As a result of its popularity, 'Jim Crow' became an adjective and the segregation statutes became known as the 'Jim Crow laws' in the 1890s (Woodward 7). This example shows that blackface and minstrelsy shows, based on the lampooning of African Americans, had become part of American cultural life. Minstrelsy was the popular form of musical theatre during the 19th century. As I will discuss in the following chapter, the minstrel shows led to stereotypical images of Black people that would burden Black performers for generations. Minstrelsy was however the path for Black artists to enter the stage (Woll 1) and despite all its degrading rituals it needs to be acknowledged as an ancestor of Black theatre, particularly of Black musical theatre.

2 Black musical theatre: From Broadway to Harlem nightclubs and back

2.1 The special role of musical theatre

When looking at performances during the Harlem Renaissance, Black musical theatre deserves special attention for several reasons. First of all, white Americans loved black music. As much as the singing black slave was a stereotypical minstrel image, talent in dance music was one of the few things that black people were recognised for. The syncopated tunes of ragtime were immensely popular from 1890. Black popular and dance music was exciting and new to the ears of white America (Riis 36-37). During the peak of the Harlem Renaissance, white people went up to Harlem "for the music and the entertainment", as Eubie Blake phrases it (cf. Huggins 339-340). Even when black theatres devoted to non-music drama emerged in Harlem, the picture of New York's black theatre scene was still dominated by musical theatre and music clubs from a white perspective (Krasner 135). Therefore, music was the Black performers' key to get the attention of a white audience.

On the other hand, musical theatre was also the genre that had to suffer the most from the legacy of Jim Crow images and derogatory minstrel stereotypes. Audiences had become attached to the minstrel shows as the earliest form of a musical revue. With the minstrel shows, they had become attached to the Negro images they presented (Hay 15). The actors of the early 20th century musicals did not mind the stereotypical images at first. The most important thing to them was that for the first time, Black artists could make a living in the performing arts (18). The minstrel label should however influence the themes and forms of musical theatre of the ensuing decades.

2.2 Vaudeville and the first black musical comedies (1880-1910)

Minstrel shows made it possible for black artists to pursue stage careers, but it also forced them to continue the genre's stereotypes as well as its forms (Woll 2). Vaudeville and variety entertainment were the link between minstrelsy and musical comedies (Riis 5). The vaudeville show, which emerged in the 1880s, resembled the minstrel show in its form: The stage show was typically composed of a number of unconnected acts, which appealed to a broad audience because of their enormous diversity (Snyder xiii-xvi). Even though the diversity lead to a more flexible format (Riis 5) blackface was still too strong a theatrical convention to allow black performers to break out of the stage stereotype (Snyder 120f.). It took big names such as Eubie Black and Noble Sissle to abandon the convention. "The Dixie Duo" was one of the first major acts to appear on stage without burnt cork makeup (Snyder 123).

There were, however, some things that did change about the perception of blacks on stage. Shows appeared that at least claimed to portray authentic black history and life. These shows were produced by whites and often rather close to minstrelsy in their forms, but they still marked an opening of audiences towards more realistic depictions of blacks. *Darkest America* was one such show (Riis 6f.). The revue-like show (9) also cast a more positive light on black artists by letting them perform as 'fine art' as operatic scenes – a contrast to the minstrel images of the dim-witted Negro (8):

> The authentic meaning of Darkest America lay in its demonstration of diverse talents ... certainly it revealed few of the quotidian realities of antebellum Southern life; but it did suggest an alternative perspective to the simplistic distorted images held by many Northerners about blacks. It showed the collective talent of black folk who had transmuted the pain of slavery into art. (Riis 8)

A few shows in the revue format followed *Darkest America*. Black artists were starting to be seen more frequently on vaudeville stages now and some of the shows had an exclusively black cast. But behind the scenes, white producers and managers were still in charge, which narrowed creativity and artistic expression immensely (Riis 11).

Composer and director Bob Cole had grown tired of being restricted and disrespected by white theatrical producers, so he broke away to write his first musical comedy and established his own production company. On 4 April, 1989, *A Trip to Coontown* opened on Broadway, the first musical comedy that was written, produced and performed by blacks. Although this certainly was a big achievement in the history of Black theatre the show still had strong similarities to early black revues and the images of Negroes that were portrayed on stage did not differ a great deal from the minstrel shows. (cf. Woll 11ff.)

The turn of the century marked the beginning of a change. As Allen Woll phrases it, "the rigid colour bar between minstrelsy and musical theatre had finally begun to collapse" (15). Bob Cole, John Rosamond Johnson and his brother James Weldon Johnson started writing songs for Broadway shows that avoided the old stereotypes and drew a more positive image of Negroes (Woll 15). "Louisiana Lize", which became integrated into the successful show *The Bell of Bridgeport,* was followed by many more hit songs. The trio began to make a full-time living out of their song-writing. From today's perspective, it is noteworthy that sheet music sales made up the largest part of the profits (Woll 17). With their increasing success on Broadway, Cole and Johnson aimed to produce musicals of higher quality that abandoned the conventional stereotypes (Woll 27). In 1909, they finally succeeded in producing such a show that was well received by the white audience and critics at the same time: *The Red Moon* (Woll 24, 27).

2.3 The Term of Exile (1910-1920)

With the disappearances of the major black Broadway stars, Cole, the Johnson brothers, Walker and Cook, black musicals also disappeared from Broadway around 1910 (Woll 50). This development allowed for black theatre to develop away from Broadway, meaning away from the limitations imposed by white audiences and critics (ibid.). Theatres catering to a black audience were now opening in Harlem (Krasner 15). But now that the constraints formerly imposed by the white audience were lifted, it was the task and the struggle of African American performers to negotiate their own definition of black theatre (cf. chapter 3).

2.4 Shuffle Along - Back to Broadway (1921-1929)

Shuffle Along by the Sissle and Blake duo brought black performance back to Broadway (Woll 57). The show opened in May 1921 at the 63rd Street Theatre. The musical became a surprise hit and was to be the most popular show of the Harlem Renaissance (Krasner 239). The music and the comedy were enjoyed by critics as well as the public (Woll 65), so it is certainly true to claim that *Shuffle Along* contributed a great part to the legitimisation of the Black musical and theatre (Woll 60). It proved that money could be made out of black entertainment, which had an effect beyond Broadway. Langston Hughes regarded *Shuffle Along* as the show that gave a "scintillating send-off to that Negro vogue in Manhattan" (qtd. in Woll 60).

In some ways, *Shuffle Along* managed to break old conventions. Critics praised the modern musical score, especially the love song "Love Will Find a Way". The popularity of the duet is all the more remarkable because love songs performed by coloured people had been a taboo until then. According to Jones, the convention was that "love songs sung by blacks had to be comic or parodic" (69). Granting blacks the right to show true emotions on stage meant a step towards accepting African Americans as equally human.

Shuffle Along is, however, also a prime example that the success of black shows always came at a price. The price that the creators of *Shuffle Along* had to pay to win the favour of the white audience was to cave in to the demand for conventional Negro images. The main characters performed in "heavy blackface makeup, spoke in fractured dialect, and performed stereotypes associated with African Americans" (Krasner 247). Ironically, the popularity of *Shuffle Along* made it the benchmark for every black show to succeed it. It "became the model by which all black musicals were judged until well into the 1930s" (Woll 75), hence bringing back the audience's expectation to see minstrel stereotypes on stage (cf. Woll 78). The same applies to its form. There was no coherent plot into which the songs were integrated, which made it reminiscent of vaudevillian revues. *Strut Miss Lizzie*, one of the first shows to follow *Shuffle Along*, even went one step back and abandoned the libretto completely (79).

It took two years until the black writers Flournoy Miller and Aubrey Lyles were successful with a show that renounced blackface and was perceived by many as "racially true" (Woll 88). *Runnin' Wild* owed its acceptance among white and black audiences to a great extent to the incorporation of the popular Charleston Dance (Woll 89ff.). Whites loved the exciting rhythms and blacks appreciated the return to "primitive Negro music" (Woll 90), which had also been the determining factor for the success of *Shuffle Along*. Blake and Sissle's hit musical had obviously brought about as many limitations to black musicals as it had provided opportunities for black artists to establish a stage career (Woll 93).

3 Black Drama: In search of the right direction

3.1 Protest drama or folk theatre?

While the black artists of the musical theatre had basically given in to the demands of commercial success there still was a factional struggle between the representatives of non-musical theatre. W. E. B. Du Bois and Alain Locke are among the most important names of the Harlem Renaissance when it comes to the theoretical considerations of Black Drama. At the same time, they are also representative of its directional problem. The point at issue was how theatre was best to be used on behalf of the Harlem Renaissance's striving for racial renewal.

On 22 October 1913, Du Bois' pageant *The Star of Ethiopia* opened. It depicted African American history in a way that differed immensely from the images that were traditionally presented on American stages at the time for Du Bois portrayed the Negro as superior and black culture as richer than that of Europe (Krasner 81f). *The Star of Ethiopia* showed "African peoples inventing everything from fire to the Sabbath" (Hay 78f.).

Propaganda to elevate instead of humiliate African Americans was a completely new concept and triggered a debate on the portrayal of the black people.

For Du Bois, theatre had to be exclusively political. He wanted to show characters and plots that portrayed the fight of the Negro against racism (Hay 3). In order to show this struggle, Du Bois believed it necessary to present an idealized image of African Americans on stage (Hay 25). He demanded characters that were "model human beings" (Hay 5) and he advocated the use of an elevated language (ibid.). Plays had to be provocative rather than to strive for recognition according to Du Bois. He wished for Protest dramas with the objective of making African Americans self-confident as a race (Hay 83). Any play that was not political and any character that did not uplift the Negro image made the white stereotypes win ground, according to Du Bois (Hay 13).

Alain Locke, on the other hand, had a different form of Black drama in mind. His Folk drama was to show authentic black characters and plots that presented "these people's 'lusty' lives, myths, legends and histories" (Hay 5). He wanted to show real people instead of idealized types even if there was the danger that they could be misunderstood by the white audiences (Hay 21). Unlike Du Bois, Locke eventually accepted that the early musicals were, despite all derogatory images, a foundation for his theatre. He advanced the view that even the clichéd depictions of African Americans developed "a positive self-respect and self-reliance" (qtd. in Hay 21). Just like blackface performers of the early 20th century, he hoped that stereotypes would eventually eradicate racial bias. Du Bois objected to this. Contrary to Locke, he was concerned that depicting realistic black characters on the commercial stage would rather amplify the old stereotypes. In his "Criteria of Negro Art", he also expressed the fear that such views deluded black artists into stopping "agitation of the Negro question" (par. 19).

The Crisis tried to answer the question "The Negro in Art: How Shall He Be Portrayed?" in 1926 by inviting major writers and producers to state their position on the matter (Scott 434). Not surprisingly, no consensus was found. This lack of a clearly defined direction might have led to the little value that is attached to the theatre of the Harlem Renaissance today and is often cited as an example for the 'failure' of that period (cf. Scott 435f.). Nevertheless, both schools brought forth important dramatists who produced a variety of portrayals of African Americans in their plays.

3.2 Folk drama and the Little Theatre movement

Many writers responded to Locke's appeal to recollect the folk roots of African American culture in the dramas and to depict a realistic image of black life on stage (Scott 429). Georgia Douglas Johnson and Willis Richardson were two representatives of folk drama writers of the 1920s. Even though they lived most parts of their lives in Washington, D.C. they are counted among the important dramatists of the Harlem Renaissance (Krasner 132). Both Richardson and Johnson wanted to create realistic representations of black people in their plays, following to Locke's definition of folk drama (Krasner 132; 135). They wanted to change the self-perception of black audiences by showing "ordinary black people" (Richardson, as qtd. in Krasner 136) and "average Negro life" (Johnson, ibid.). Therefore, their plays were mainly fitted to and performed for black audiences and did not win recognition among whites.

Although Johnson and Richardson mainly followed Locke's view on Black theatre they both integrated Du Bois' idea that drama should serve as propaganda (Krasner 136). Richardson clearly stated that he aimed to bring about social change with his plays and "to gain sympathy" for the African American struggle among audiences that had not been familiar with the issue (Krasner 151f.). Johnson wanted to enhance the prestige of African Americans (Krasner 137) and her anti-lynching dramas were obviously written for propaganda purposes (Krasner 152).

The writers who created plays against the notion of the mainstream theatres on Broadway formed part of the so-called "Little Theatre Movement", which arose around 1917 (Krasner 137). The disappointment with Broadway productions that were full of minstrelsy stereotypes and the on-going debate about the meaning of black drama led to the establishment of smaller, more experimental theatres in Harlem, Greenwich Village and also in Washington and Chicago (Krasner 208f.). The main aim of the Black Little Theatre Movement was to abandon all remainders of the minstrel past and instead to portray "the reality of the black experience" (Krasner 210). As a result numerous small theatres and black companies developed, among them Du Bois' Krigwa Theatre, the Hapgood Players, the Lincoln Theatres and many more venues in Harlem. Most of these groups were short-lived and none of them were commercially successful. The productions were designed to work within the African American community, so they hardly attracted any attention outside their own scene (Krasner 211). Even among African Americans there was no support for the experimental political plays: "Mass audiences, Black or white, still tended to choose entertainment over uplift, and entertainment usually meant clinging to images fixed in the past" (Scott 434).

It is difficult to judge the importance of the Little Theatre dramas of the period 1918-1927. Du Bois, Locke and other intellectuals sought to encourage and promote black writers by publishing them in their books, offering contests in their magazines and providing them opportunities to perform in their theatres (Krasner 237). Without a doubt, these efforts resulted in numerous dramas that dealt with the important questions of racial identity and image. Their plays did, however, not affect the public interest in the cause, neither among blacks nor among whites. The Little Theatre groups went unrecognised in comparison with the Broadway shows.

3.3 Black drama on Broadway

Compared to musical theatre, there were only a few Black non-musical plays that made an appearance on Broadway. The first drama written by a Black playwright was *The Chipwoman's Fortune* in 1923. Although it was praised by the critics for its realistic view on black life the play never became a crowd puller and playwright Willis Richardson did not make his career (Scott 430f.).

Porgy, which opened in October 1927, was praised by black journalists of *Opportunity* as well as by white critics of *The New York Times* enthusiastically as "the most innovative production" (Lewis 207). Porgy was proudly regarded as 'Harlem's play'. It played, however, to Broadway audiences and it was only middle-class Broadway audiences who could afford to see it (ibid.). This of course conflicted with the intention to use theatre as a means of strengthening racial self-confidence but *Porgy* is still regarded as one of the biggest successes of the Harlem Renaissance when it comes to its public image.

The next Harlem play to be performed on Broadway was *Meek Mose* by Frank Wilson in 1928. The black community was too content to see yet another "Negro" production on Broadway to mind the "extreme racial stereotyping" of the play (Lewis 207). But it becomes apparent that commercial successes directly entailed compromises on political correctness. One year later, the melodrama *Harlem* was indeed praised by some black critics for its social realism, but it still focussed on those aspects of Negro life "that would not destabilize mainstream views ... of the 1920s" (Miller 91). Non-musical plays suffered the same setbacks as the musical comedies: Broadway and the commercial stage were not the place for political propaganda.

4 Dilemmas of the Black performer: dangers and chances of going mainstream

4.1 The double audience

The abstract of the history of Black theatre shows that the main dilemma black writers and producers were faced with was whether to please the "overwhelmingly white audience" or to write for the Black community, which demanded to see a new image of the Negro, but was not able to offer the same material compensation (Scott 433). James Weldon-Johnson describes this dilemma as the problem of the double audience:

> It is a divided audience ... made up of two elements with differing and often opposite and antagonistic points of view. His audience is always both white America and black America. The moment a Negro writer takes up his pen or sits down to his typewriter he is immediately called upon to solve, consciously or unconsciously, this problem of the double audience. To whom shall he address himself, to his own black group or to white America? (477)

The double audience was a dilemma for black writers in general, but it was even more essential for playwrights and theatre producers, whose survival depended directly on the approval of their (double) audience. When discussing the potential of Shuffle Along, Lester A. Walton stated in the New York Age that a Black show needed to present certain "stage types" like "the old mammy and Uncle Joe variety and blackfaced comedians" to be popular among white audiences (qtd. in Krasner 246). These stage types obviously conflicted with the interests of the black theatregoers.

Not only did black performances have to please a double-audience but they also had to face two groups of reviewers. Attempts to abandon white conventions were usually received with taunting disapproval by white critics (Woll 78). *Put and Take*, the first black Broadway show to follow *Shuffle Along*, was excoriated. One review claimed that the revue was vainly trying to shine "in dress suits when it should have been a success in plantation jumpers" and demanded that black performers "should remain different, distinct, and indigenous" (Woll 77f.). Not surprisingly, the adaptation to white expectations was ridiculed by black critics. *Harlem* was the only Black drama that was commercially successful on Broadway, but the majority of Black critics objected to the way that stereotypes were propagated on stage (Scott 438).

The dilemma of the double audience could not be resolved. To achieve the first aim of the Harlem Renaissance, a change in the mental attitude towards the African American race, the black artists needed to present their plays and shows to the white public. Gearing performances towards white audiences, however, meant that the plays had to cater to the tastes of the target group, which meant conforming to stereotypical conventions. The clichéd portrayals of African Americans conflicted in turn with the second objective of the Harlem Renaissance: a new racial pride in order to "uplift" the community's identity.

4.2 Imitating white material or creating new black material

The moral of Will Marion Cook's Broadway production *Jes' Lak White Fo'ks* is that the black people should find happiness in their own culture instead of trying to imitate the culture of the whites (Woll 10). This describes exactly another dilemma that Black artists were caught in. When black Broadway productions, which were mainly exposed to and dependent on the judgment of whites, tried to abandon old conventions they were dismissed as not authentically black. Coles and Johnson's most advanced work *The Shoo-Fly Regiment*, which premiered in 1907, was dismissed by white critics as too imitative of white productions (Woll 23f.). When Bert Williams and George Walker produced *Abyssinia* (1906) in an attempt to leave minstrel images behind, the *Theatre Magazine* scathed it as "a white man's show acted by coloured men" (Woll 45f.).

Even the hit musical *Shuffle Along* was blamed for copying white performance in a few cases. Percy Hammond wrote in 1922 that the performers were just "imitating ... a mediocre musical comedy as it would be done by mediocre white performers" (qtd. in Woll 71). For the next big musical by Sissle and Blake, *The Chocolate Dandies* (1924), the reviews were more explicit. White critics disapproved of its ambition to perform "'white folks' material" (Woll 91f.). Black reviewers simultaneously criticised that it lacked elements that were distinctive of the black racial community (Woll 92). This dilemma proofed to be irresolvable for black producers: a show could be either too stereotypical or 'not black enough'; an in-between did not seem to exist.

4.3 White writers and producers staging "black" drama

It is significant that only five black playwrights reached Broadway during the Harlem Renaissance while several white writers were extremely successful with their depictions of Black life (Scott 438). African American actors benefitted from the interest of white playwrights in the black community as black characters were no longer played by white actors in blackface but more and more replaced by black actors. For instance in Ridgely Torrence's *Three Plays for a Negro Theatre*, which opened in April 1917, a company of black artists participated onstage as well as backstage as costume and stage designers. This meant of course that completely unfounded and tasteless minstrel portrayals were slowly abandoned. It does not alter the fact, however, that the Negro was still shown on stage in the way he was perceived by whites, namely white playwrights (Scott 429).

The same applies to the funding of black shows. Apart from the contests that *Crisis* and *Opportunity* organised to promote black dramatists, there was neither financial funding nor an institutional structure to nurture black works (Scott 436). The consequence was that black artists had to rely on white producers. This was especially the case for the high-budget Broadway musicals. It was a surprise to many that the producer of the most successful Broadway revues was white (Woll 97f.): Lew Leslie produced and directed among others *Plantation Revue* (1922), *Dixie to Broadway* (1924), which was the big breakthrough for Florence Mills, and *Blackbirds of 1928*. Leslie's formula for success was firstly "to discover and exploit new black talent" (Woll 98) like Florence Mills or Lena Horne. He also cashed in on white New York's interest in everything black by integrating images of the New Negro and elements of the Harlem vogue into his shows (Woll 110f.).

Lew Leslie's production made it possible for numerous black artists to start their stage careers, but at the same time his strong influence converted the black musical revue "almost entirely from a black to white-controlled enterprise" (Woll 113). Furthermore, due to the success of Leslie's revue shows, black shows had almost exclusively gone back to the revue form in the late 1920s. The loss of financial control led to the black artists losing creative control and opportunities for blacks to exert influence on stage portrayals of their own race were still non-existent at the end of the 1920s (Woll 81; 134).

4.4 Segregation and discrimination

It is often forgotten that the black performer also depended on the approval of white audiences because audiences of the major venues were almost exclusively white (Woll 72). In the early 1920s, segregation was still the rule in New York's theatres, which meant that seating for blacks was restricted to the balcony (ibid.). The discrimination extended beyond Broadway. Even in some Harlem clubs, black people would not be allowed admission. One of the most famous examples is the Cotton Club, a night club in uptown Manhattan that was well-known for its whites-only policy (cf. Huggins 340; Jerving). These cases demonstrate once more the strong influence of white managers and producers on supposedly 'black' entertainment.

Shuffle Along achieved to bring about some tangible changes in the seating policy in 1921. The show was able to attract a larger black audience as they offered some late performances that allowed people with longer working hours to attend the theatre. In addition, black members of the audience were allowed to sit in the orchestra for the first time. (Woll 71f.) A white critic was surprised that "coloured patrons were noticed as far front as the fifth row" (Woll 72). Even if two thirds of the orchestra seats were still exclusively for whites (ibid.) the liberalisation of the seating policies can certainly be regarded as one of the palpable political changes that has to be credited to black musical theatre.

The segregation policies were, however, not completely lifted throughout the Harlem Renaissance. As late as 1929, Wallace Thurman, the co-author of the success play *Harlem*, was not permitted to sit in the white section of the theatre (Scott 438). This is all the more remarkable as it was his own play that was being performed that night.

Conclusion

Hindsight is marvellous. When Larry Neal assesses that the Harlem Renaissance was "essentially a failure" (39), he does so from a 1960s perspective. In retrospect, it might seem that the performers of the Harlem Renaissance contributed little to establish a black community within white America (cf. Neal 39). But such a view disregards the circumstances and prior conditions under which the Harlem Renaissance took place. With the legacy of minstrelsy and blackface stereotypes, the artists at the beginning of the 19th century had more to rid themselves of than the figures of the Black Arts Movement did. Instead of comparing the two movements, it would be more appropriate to see the Harlem Renaissance and its performing art as a ground-breaking preliminary stage.

Although Du Bois and Locke advanced different views on the direction of Black theatre, they both agreed on one thing: Broadway musicals were not the appropriate form to mediate political themes (Hay 20ff.). Their contempt for musical theatre, which, in opposition to the New Negro movement, was still rife with derogatory Negro images, is comprehensible. Nevertheless, we should not forget that the small successes of Black 'political theatre' were only possible because commercial Broadway shows had initialised a legitimisation of Black theatre in the first place. The Harlem Renaissance would not have been the same without the initial popularity of Black Broadway musical shows. White New York would not have shown the same interest in Harlem had it not acquired a taste for Black music and entertainment on Broadway (Lewis 164).

Even if Broadway was still "entranced" with the old stereotypes in 1937 (Krasner 8), it would be negligent not to recognize that black artists had come a long way. The debates of Locke, Du Bois, Johnson and other Harlem Renaissance theorists demonstrate that African Americans strived for the modernisation of black theatre. The popularity of black musical shows showed that black performers could reach a white audience. Musical composers as well as some playwrights had tried to make the connection between modernisation and Broadway audiences. Even though those tries were generally dismissed by the public they were small steps to a renewal of black theatre.

The mainstream discussion is the wrong approach to judge the Harlem Renaissance theatre insofar as black artists did not have the choice: They did not deliberately cash in on the presentation of derogatory Negro images, thereby betraying the cause of the New Negro movement. Their only 'failure' was that they were not able to completely abandon the deadlocked conventions that had established over the decades preceding the Harlem Renaissance. In the light of the barriers and dilemmas that were merely conditioned by the circumstances of their period, this was an unsolvable task. Particularly through the comparison of the successful Broadway Black musical comedies and the short-lived but political Black dramas it becomes obvious that producers could either aim for one or the other. Commercial success and broad audiences were evidently not compatible with the creation of a new racial identity through meaningful performances.

Works cited

Baker, Houston A. *Modernism and the Harlem Renaissance*. Chicago : University of Chicago Press, 1987. Print.

Buck, Christopher. "Harlem Renaissance." Ed. Leslie M. Alexander & Walter C. Rucker. *Encyclopedia of African American History* 2010 : 795-799. Print.

Du Bois, W.E.B. "Criteria of Negro Art." *The Crisis* 32.October (1926): 290-297. Print.

Hay, Samuel A. *African American Theatre*. Cambridge : Cambridge University Press, 1994. Print.

Huggins, Nathan Irvin. "Interview with Eubie Blake, October 16, 1973." *Voices from the Harlem Renaissance*. New York: Oxford University Press, 1976. 336-340. Print.

Jerving, Ryan. "Cotton Club." Ed. Cary D. Wintz & Paul Finkelm. *Encyclopedia of the Harlem Renaissance* 2004. Web. 21 Mar. 2012.

Johnson, James Weldon. "The Dilemma of the Negro Author." *The American Mercury* 15.60 (1928): 477–481. Print.

Jones, John Bush. *Our Musicals, Ourselves: a Social History of the American Musical Theatre*. UPNE, 2003. Print.

Kenrick, John. "A History of the Musical: Minstrel Shows." *musicals101.com*. 2003. Web. 21 Mar. 2012.

Lewis, David L. *When Harlem Was in Vogue*. New York: Knopf, 1981. Print.

Mahar, William John. Behind the Burnt Cork Mask: Early Blackface Minstrelsy and Antebellum American Popular Culture. University of Illinois Press, 1999. Print.

Miller, Henry D. *Theorizing Black Theatre: Art Versus Protest in Critical Writings, 1898-1965*. McFarland, 2010. Print.

Neal, Larry. "The Black Arts Movement." *The Drama Review: TDR* 12.4 (1968): 29-39. Web. 22 Mar. 2012.

Riis, Thomas L. *More Than Just Minstrel Shows*. New York: Inst. of Studies in American Music, 1992. Print.

Scott, Freda L. "Black Drama and the Harlem Renaissance." *Theatre Journal* 37.4 (1985): 426-439. Web. 20 Mar. 2012.

Snyder, Robert W. *The Voice of the City: Vaudeville and Popular Culture in New York*. New York ; Oxford: Oxford Univeristy Press, 1989. Print.

Woll, Allen L. *Black Musical Theatre*. Baton Rouge, LA : Louisiana State University Press, 1989. Print.

Woodward, Comer Vann. *The Strange Career of Jim Crow*. Oxford University Press, 1955. Print.